THE
BOTTOM LINE
A Lighthearted Look at Accountancy

THE BOTTOM LINE

A Lighthearted Look at Accountancy

PETER VAINES
WITH ROGER NUTTALL

DIXON WILSON

DW

CENTENARY
1888-1988

Published to celebrate the centenary of
Dixon Wilson - Chartered Accountants

Macdonald
Queen Anne Press

A *Queen Anne Press* Book

©Queen Anne Press 1988

Introduction ©Peter Vaines 1988

First published in Great Britain in 1988 by
Queen Anne Press, a division of
Macdonald & Co (Publishers) Ltd
3rd Floor
Greater London House
Hampstead Road
London
NW1 7QX

A member of Maxwell Pergamon Publishing Corporation plc

Jacket illustrations Front: Kevin Woodcock
                     Back: Ken Pyne (*Private Eye*)

British Library Cataloguing in Publication Data

The Bottom Line.
  1. Accounting – Anecdotes, facetiae, satire, etc.
  I. Vaines, Peter
  657'.0207   HF5657

  ISBN 0 356 15538 2

Typeset by Betagraphics, Midsomer Norton, Bath, Avon

Printed and bound in Great Britain by The Bath Press

CONTENTS

To Stella

Peter Vaines' royalties are being donated to the Sunshine Fund for Blind Babies and Young Children.

I am indebted to all those who have contributed stories from their own experience either as accountants in the profession or in industry, as well as those who have benefited from or suffered at the hands of accountants, auditors and the tax man. They include:

A.G. Bazell, George Bogle, John Bibby, Gyles Brandreth, Michael Checkland, John Cope, Richard Eyre, Barry Fantoni, Alex Graham, Charlotte Gower, Sir Geoffrey Howe, Ludovic Kennedy, Griff Rhys Jones, Baroness Phillips, Patrick Philips, Jack Purvis, Alec Poole, Basil Sabine, Chris Thomas, John Whiter, Robin Williamson, John Mason, Francis Flynn, Reg Taylor, Peter Thomas, David Taylor, Harry Cohen, Chris de Glanville and all my partners and colleagues for their help – not forgetting all those who tried but failed to think of anything amusing.

Special thanks are due to Amanda Schlagman who patiently typed draft after draft without a word of complaint; my wife Stella who spent hours of research in professional libraries into the minutiae of accounts and accountants (which will be universally recognised as a task considerably beyond the call of any duty) and finally to Barbara Levy without whose faith and encouragement this would never have started.

INTRODUCTION

THE BOTTOM LINE

ACCOUNTANT WITH A SENSE OF HUMOUR–PLEASE LOVE ME

A humorous book on accounts or accountancy may be thought of as a task of Herculean proportions and when I was asked to compile this book my reaction was the same as everybody else's – you have to be joking. Indeed, the best joke was thought to be that anybody could imagine that humour could be found in accountancy – which everybody knows is dull and boring.

Other professions, notably Medicine, the Church and the Law, have generated considerable humour for centuries but accountancy has suffered from what the marketing men might call 'poor image projection.' Celebrities and others in the public eye are often called upon for a few *bons mots* on diverse subjects and can usually be relied on for some witty anecdote. However, when it comes to accountancy a kind of grey mist descends and humour goes out of the window. This is perhaps exemplified by the view expressed by Ludovic Kennedy who was kind enough to write to me explaining that in 50 years' experience, he had

> **Never found anything remotely amusing about accountancy or Income Tax**

and he is not the only one. Even Gyles Brandreth, a veritable doyen of professional humour, told me that although his life has been a riot of hilarity throughout its span, his experience with accountancy had been

> **utterly bereft of the least glimmer of amusement.**

Griff Rhys Jones admitted that the whole matter caused him nothing but grief. The whole project therefore seemed somewhat unpromising – not to say doomed from the start.

'That's my advice as your accountant. Speaking as your friend, I'd have to say it was pretty lousy advice.'

'So you want to contact your accountant whose name is Peter and he passed away last week.'

However, on further reflection there seemed to be at least the potential for some amusement. Accountants occupy a highly privileged position in the lives of their clients because they are privy to their financial affairs. People are funny about money and would never dream of disclosing anything about their savings or earnings to anybody else – sometimes not even their spouse. But once inside an accountant's office a strange intimacy occurs and they reveal all – as if they were talking to a doctor. Such intimacy gives rise to a great deal of humour and some of these experiences are recounted in this book. However, it is inevitable that the demands of confidentiality means that the best of these anecdotes often have to remain anonymous.

It seems that literature has not entirely overlooked the existence of accountants and their chosen field of activity, and throughout this book will be found views on the subject by numerous literary characters. Even the Pope is reported to have a kind word to say about tax advisers.

'Typical accountant! Always looks at the bottom line first.'

My own path towards accountancy was relatively conventional – I just drifted into it like everybody else. Although my father was an accountant, I never was entirely clear about what accountancy was nor what accountants did. I was brought up knowing that there were three types of accountant – 'Chartered', 'Certified' and 'Turf' – but the distinction between them was never made clear.

Throughout my childhood I never tired of hearing a story about my parents' early married life. Just like every newly qualified accountant my father maintained meticulous records of the household income and expenditure and after the first two months he was able to draw some unfavourable conclusions – the expenditure was consistently higher than the income. Action was urgently required so he took my mother through the figures and at the end gently inquired of her what action they should take to remedy the potentially disastrous situation. 'I think,' she said, 'we must stop keeping these records'.

This does seem to be no less pragmatic an approach than that of Samuel Pepys' wife. He records in his diary:

> Coming home tonight I did go to examine my wife's accounts and finding things that seemed somewhat doubtful I was angry though she did make it pretty plain; but confessed that when she do miss a sum she do add something to other things to make it.

KEVIN WOODCOCK

What an extraordinary idea!

The international opportunities for accountants attract many to the profession, because the language of numbers is almost universal; there is thought to be scope for spreading the accounting gospel to all parts of the world. The reality is not always as charming as it appears. The opportunities for chartered accountants in Nice, St Tropez, Gstaad and Barbados (in sequence of course) is extremely limited and indeed some countries have a most unorthodox approach to accounting accuracy and procedure – not to say personal security. A colleague of mine, upon qualification, was extremely keen to take up a post in a sun-soaked foreign island but rapidly went off the idea when he came to the part which promised him (among other delights) a 24-hour armed guard.

In some areas they are much more civilized, it being reported that in one country the local priest is always asked to bless the union of the new auditor and his client, the feelings of the outgoing auditor being soothed by a present from the incoming auditor. Such presents are said to vary from a couple of donkeys to the eldest daughter of the incoming auditor. That certainly seems to be a good way to avoid some awkward outgoing auditor making representations at the Annual General Meeting.

BEGINNINGS

Roger Nuttall

Who is to blame for inventing accountancy? There are claimants –
or, rather disclaimants. As soon as one historian thinks he has found
the source of this river of financial finagling, another paddles up an
unexplored tributary and discovers a prior claim.

For many years – and for want of anybody better – Fra Luca
Pacioli has held the title of *Fons et Origo*. He was a good, romantic
figure to pick on: probably born in Tuscany (where a tax-dodging
tradition of creative accounting continues to this day), later lecturing
on mathematics at the world's great universities and becoming a
professor at Pisa.

One of the few solid things we know about Fra Luca is that he
was up to no good in 1493; perhaps he took a view on what
Columbus' discovery a year earlier would do to the gold market, and
traded on inside information. Whatever the reason, we know that he
was recalled to Assisi under threat of excommunication.

Other than that, Fra Luca's life is fogged by time, *caveats* and im-
precisions. In spite of that, accountants regard him as their founder.
Or because of it.

Be that as it may, he was born some time after 1445, died
some time after 1515, and is regarded as the man who made
the most significant contribution to the duplicitous art of double
entry book-keeping. He published a treatise on the subject in Venice
and there are passing references to the subject in some of his
other works.

But his greatest publication – *Suma de Arithmetica Geometria
Proportioni et Proportioni* – is a work of pure mathematics. You can
see a picture of Fra Luca with his work in a Naples museum.

By all means, let us praise (or revile) Fra Luca. But who can
imagine a business without books of record? And can there be books
without a book-keeper? Long before Fra Luca, practical traders and
civil servants had developed their own rough-and-ready accounting
systems; traces of them survive in archaeological records, and early
documents.

Some sort of accountancy seems to have been going on in the
Babylon of 2000BC. Soon afterwards, the Chinese and the Egyptians
were at it.

By 1500BC, animal food costs were being recorded and analysed
by Sumerians in a way many modern farmers would recognise; on
the other side of the world, Mandarins of the Chou dynasty were

K. Lamb

developing a simple version of the Source and Application of Funds Statement, which still lies at the heart of much corporate accountancy.

The foundations of foreign currency accounting were laid in Athens, around 418BC. The public spending records of that time show surprising sophistication in handling and reconciling the foreign money that went in and out of the City's treasury.

Meanwhile, halfway up the Andes, the Incas were quietly getting on with inventing what many would see as the true beginning of modern accountancy. It was called Quipua, or Qiupu (then, as now, accountants were better at counting than writing). It consisted of keeping and reconciling accounts on long tangles of string tied in surprising places. Anybody who has ever filled up a tax return will recognise that.

Another sign of a maturing profession came in the Greece of 400BC, or thereabouts, when the first known accountancy dispute came to court. Like modern cases of the same kind, it began well, dealing with great and important questions of principle, but degenerated into an unseemly squabble over details.

The dispute concerned the children of Diodetus, who had been killed in action seeing off the Spartans, or maybe the Egyptians; court cases never tell us the interesting bits. Diodetus' brother Diogeiton was appointed trustee to his two young nephews, who were due to come into a useful sum of money when they came of age. However,

'. . . halfway up the Andes . . . long tangles of string tied in surprising places.'

when they finally got their hands on it, there was less than they thought. Looking for someone to blame, they settled on poor Diogeiton, claiming that he had overstated the expense of bringing them up, and pocketed the difference.

Diogeiton replied with a phrase as familiar now as it was then, allowing a little latitude in translation: 'You can't imagine how much it costs to raise two growing boys'. And he produced detailed accounts to prove it.

That was where the argument began to degenerate. The court spent hours listening to orators thrashing out thorny questions like the price of a haircut, and how frequently a fashionable boy should have it done. (This remains a contentious matter in modern, teenager-containing households.) However, the case did not advance the cause of accounting history very far.

Oddly, we have little notion of how the Romans went about their financial control and accountancy. It must have been highly advanced, for some of their great business ventures (like mining partnerships) resembled modern multi-nationals so closely as makes no difference. Moreover, their unified tax and army pay systems – consistent from the Scottish border to Egypt, and from Spain to the Caucasus – must have included detailed controls to ensure that most of the right money got into the right hands at the right time. Did we but know it, there were probably proto-accountants in Bethlehem counting the House of David and working out their code numbers when Jesus was born.

Yet the only thing we know – and that uncertainly – is that the Romans used a primitive form of double entry, more than a millenium before Fra Luca. They preferred to use slaves to do the accounting (some articled clerks would say that hasn't changed).

For accountants, the Dark Ages were – well, dark. Who looked after the Roman asset write-offs for the Vikings? Who depreciated the depredations of the Vandals? Who trial-balanced for the tribes of the North? In monasteries and courts, the esoteric skills must have been handed on generation to generation, like the arts of bowmaking or boiling a boar. Occasionally the fog lifts a little, as in the Domesday Book (which can be regarded as a thorough asset revaluation of a newly-acquired subsidiary, partly carried out to make the assets work harder, and partly to provide suitable incentive bonuses).

When the mists finally part, in the Renaissance, accountancy comes into view as a fully fledged trade, if not yet a profession.

'. . . the Romans . . . preferred to use slaves to do the accounting . . .'

One example is enough to make the point. In the Genoa archives for March 1340 (still a century before Fra Luca) rests the Massari ledger, a day-to-day record of deals done by one of the great trading houses of the time. We can follow one deal through in detail over a period of eight months. It started when Massari bought 80 one hundred-pound lots of pepper for 1,940 libre. By the time they closed the deal, in November, they were 149 libre down on the deal, and (I imagine) moaning about it to all and sundry.

In the intervening months, and without difficulty, we can track the following events: the pepper price fluctuated, but ended two libre down; there were heavy tax demands on the stock of pepper; one sale was disputed and ended with Massari allowing a credit for damaged peppercorns; and the dockers demanded – and got – more than had been allowed for to shift the lots.

'. . . the pepper price fluctuated . . .'

Modern financial market supervisors find present-day share transactions shrouded more opaquely than that. Moreover, the whole record is consistently written in an early form of double entry.

Some historians, incidentally, see the whole transaction as something even more modern: a device to avoid falling foul of the authorities. How, they argue, could such a skilled and profitable house as the Massari read the pepper market so wrongly? What they were really doing was to create a 'dummy' transaction to hide a loan on which they received interest (which was then illegal).

If so, mid-14th century accounting was not only mature, but creative. When Fra Luca came along, all he did was to publish an account of what was already common practice. Moreover, as one later commentator points out, Fra Luca's methods are all very well, but in his chapter on running a shop, he suggests no way of determining whether you are making a profit or a loss. Another century passed before Jan Ympyn of Antwerp let traders into that secret. Or had they worked it out for themselves long before?

THROUGH A GLASS, DARKLY – OR HOW OTHERS SEE THE ACCOUNTANT

Accountants do not get a good press. Only actuaries fare worse: an actuary, it is said, is a man who would find accountancy too stimulating.

Whether we like it or not, the general perception of accountants is that they are dull and boring, and that accountancy is the intra-terrestrial equivalent of a black hole – figuratively speaking. In a Monty Python sketch, for example, Mr Anchovy, a chartered accountant, seeks a more interesting job, but without success.

> **Well yes Mr Anchovy but in your report here it says that you are an extremely dull person. Our experts describe you as an appallingly dull fellow, unimaginative, timid, lacking in initiative, spineless, easily dominated, no sense of humour, tedious company and irresponsibly drab and awful. Whereas in most professions these would be considerable drawbacks, in accountancy they are a positive boon.**

'No, I'm just like this at weekends – the rest of the week I'm an accountant bored out of his skull!'

*'For God's sake Denis we're on holiday!
Can't you forget you're an accountant?'*

It's no use complaining. To laymen, accountants mean tax, and looking for mistakes in the accounts, and death duties. Accountants do not send us on our way through life with a merry song and a spring in our heel; they remind us of dour realities that we would rather forget.

'I'm sorry, Mr Crossley, I'm afraid that's not
the sort of suit we're looking for.'

Lawyers fight our battles, and sometimes win. Doctors and surgeons patch us up and make us feel better. Architects – sometimes – design beautiful buildings. And we rarely meet actuaries, thank heavens.

But the world is full of accountants. And the best they can do (so it seems to their clients) is help you keep some money you thought was yours anyway. Then they charge half of that as a fee.

No use an accountant fighting back, either. If he points out that one of our leading alternative comedians is an accountant – as are two ministers of the Crown and a whole raft of top industrialists – someone will point out that, strictly, they are *ex-accountants*. There is no answer to that.

Small wonder that references to the profession in literature are sparse, and generally unfavourable. Take it on trust that there must be another side to their character; after all, somebody married most of them. With that in mind, see what others have said:

RAYMOND CHANDLER

He was a long, stooped, yellow-faced man with high shoulders, bristly eyebrows and almost no chin. The upper part of his face meant business. The lower part was just saying goodbye . . . He was a Certified Public Accountant and looked it every inch. He had ink on his fingers and there were pencils in the pocket of his open vest.

CHARLES DICKENS

In *Nicholas Nickleby*, Dickens writes of Nicholas, clearly with a sympathetic pen, that

During the next two weeks all his spare hours late at night and early in the morning were incessantly devoted to acquiring the mysteries of bookkeeping and other forms of mercantile account.

But although Dickens seems to regard the study of accountancy as a worthy activity, his view of the final product clearly does not come up to expectations. He describes accountants as 'Meek men hunched over dusty ledgers, perched on high stools, peering beneath green eyeshades'.

MARK McCORMACK (lawyer and sports entrepreneur)

In his book *What They Don't Teach You at Harvard Business School* McCormack recounts the story of the Ford Motor Company. At one time it contained a disproportionate number of accountants, and their influence was equally disproportionate. They were able to show in graphic detail that various plants were unprofitable. They were duly closed down. At a board meeting a proposal was put forward for still further plant closures and the accountants' figures were so grim and so compelling that nobody felt able to speak up. Finally an old Ford veteran said 'Why don't we close down all the plants, then we will really start to save some money?'

ELBERT HUBBARD

A man past middle age, spare, wrinkled, intelligent, cold, passive, non-committal, with eyes like a cod fish. Polite in contact but at the same time unresponsive, calm and damnably composed as a concrete post or a plaster-of-paris cast – a mere petrification with a heart of feldspar and without charm of the friendly germ, minus bowels, passion or sense of humour. Happily they never reproduce and all of them finally go to hell.

NICOLAS STACEY (Merger specialist and historian)

Although his criticism is somewhat more elegant, the message from Mr Stacey in his book *A Study in Social and Economic History 1800–1954* is equally plain:

It is not to decry or belittle members of a great profession when I confess that what, above all considerations, prompted me to embark upon writing this historical study, has been the desire to draw attention to the limited intellectual development of the profession.

'I often think how nice it would be to have enough imagination to live in a dream world.'

LORD MANCROFT

Lord Mancroft – who might have become an accountant had not six months spent adding up the petty cash book in an attic of the Midland Bank persuaded him otherwise – has a theory as to why the profession has achieved such pre-eminence in national life.

> In English law a man, with one exception, is deemed to be innocent until he is proved guilty. The exception lies of course in the tax laws where the fisc regards every taxpayer as a crook until he has established his innocence. And this, despite the fact

that judge after judge has told us that we are entitled so to arrange our affairs that the taxman's shovel digs no further into our granary than is legally preventable.

So to help their shovellers along the Treasury drafts Finance Bills of such mind-boggling complexity that you can't possibly get the shovellers off your premises without the help of a lot of very expensive accountants.

'Our fee may seem a trifle high this year, but we're trying for the Guinness Book of Records.'

WALTER BAGEHOT (Historian)

I have devoted my time for the last four months nearly exclusively to the art of book-keeping by double entry, the theory of which is agreeable, but the practice perhaps as horrible as anything ever was. I maintain in vain that sums are matters of opinion but the people in command here do not comprehend . . . and try to prove that figures tend to one result more than another, which I find myself to be false as they always come different. But there is no influencing the instinctive dogmatism of the uneducated mind.

'So I said, "Luigi, I'd rather be dead than keep two sets of books".'

GEORGE DE MARE (Industrialist)

In his book *Communicating at the Top*, George de Mare describes various styles of personal correspondence and claims to have discovered the following accountant's love letter:

Dear Mary

As stated in my previous letter dated 3 March 1982 I should greatly appreciate your consideration of certain matters discussed by us on the last occasion of our mutual propinquity.

You may remember that we agreed that our previous conferences had led us to believe that there is a substantial basis for a continued and perhaps fruitful series of meetings in which a fundamental co-operation might, eventually, on a long term consideration, result in a possible future legal status.

Nothing has come to my attention which precludes such a possibility and I therefore look forward to hearing from you at an early opportunity, remaining,

Very truly yours

John

LAWYERS

For years there has been a traditional rivalry between the accountancy and legal professions which makes lawyers unlikely to win the prize as our number one fans. However, it is pleasing to discover that not all lawyers think ill of accountants. A clue to the feelings of solicitors was revealed in the Law Society's *Gazette* of 18 March 1987.

> Solicitors are very slow and very expensive. By contrast the chartered accountant is brisk and businesslike. He may be expensive but his clients appreciate what he does for them. They cannot challenge his bill either. They cannot go to a new auditor without getting professional clearance from the original one. The chartered accountant is the shield between the client and the Inland Revenue and he can add up.

I did, however, receive one exceptionally cryptic contribution from a solicitor who always advised his clients never to see their accountants on a Wednesday as they would otherwise spoil two whole weekends.

However, accountants are not the only ones who can charge high fees.

A chartered accountant awoke one morning and ran himself a bath but no sooner had he turned on the tap full bore, when it came off in his hand. The water was pouring in and even with the plug out the level was rising. He started bailing the water out with a bucket but realising that this was getting him nowhere he rang the emergency plumber. The plumber arrived in a matter of minutes, immediately diagnosed the problem, mended the tap and restored life to normal. He explained that it was his practice to issue his bills immediately and accordingly wrote out a bill for £30. The accountant looked at his watch and calculated that as the job took only 10 minutes this was a rate of pay of £180 per hour.

'Do you know,' he said to the plumber, 'that this bill charges your time at the rate of £180 per hour? I am a chartered accountant in private practice and I cannot charge anybody anything like £180 per hour.'

'I know,' said the plumber. 'When I was a chartered accountant in private practice I couldn't charge £180 per hour either.'

THE JUDICIAL VIEW

It is often said that the views of judges do not correspond with those of ordinary people despite their efforts to put themselves in the position of the man on the Clapham omnibus. In terms of the public perception of auditors and their duty, Lord Justice Lindley in the celebrated case of *In re London and General Bank*, could hardly be further adrift. In 1895 he said of auditors:

It is no part of an auditor's duty to give advice either to directors or shareholders as to what they ought to do.

And further:
He [the auditor] does not guarantee that the books do correctly show the true position of the company's affairs.

These statements may well be technically accurate but they can hardly be said to represent the contemporary view of the auditor, a position unfortunately often held – as the following tale illustrates – in low esteem.

An old-fashioned Yorkshire businessman (famous for conducting board meetings with his three sons on the basis of 'three in favour, one against – the proposal is defeated') asked a young auditor to attend a board meeting. After keeping quiet for an hour the auditor

*'Before you jump would you care to recommend our
firm to your next of kin?'*

thought he'd better make some sort of contribution and made a harmless remark about the company's stock valuation. He was met with a frosty glare and summarily dismissed with 'shut up lad, tha's nowt but the scorer'.

Finally, the farmer's view, from Henry Brewis in the *Farming Press*.

He sits at his desk with his horn-rimmed specs
doing sums on a calculator
and come rain or shine you know bloody fine
there's a bill to pay sooner or later
he adds and subtracts and works out your tax
messing about with the figures
you've done fairly well so how in the hell
is that overdraft still gettin' bigger
those accounts are too much it's all double dutch
so you 'phone up for him to explain
but his cute office bird says haven't you heard
he's away to his villa in Spain . . .

The last word on the public perception of accountants (in their capacity as tax consultants) must go to His Holiness Pope John Paul II speaking to the Second Congress of Tax Consultants in Rome in November 1980:

May God assist you in your work as counsellors and defenders of justice.

ACCOUNTANTS AT WAR

THE BOTTOM LINE

Roger Nuttall

There is something bizarre, ludicrous even, about the notion of accountants in khaki, performing deeds of financial valour under enemy fire. Yet old sweats of the Royal Army Pay Corps – effectively the accounting branch of the Army – have many a tale of derring-do to tell. Most extraordinary of all was what happened after the fall of Singapore, early in 1942.

As the Japanese raced down the Malayan peninsula, most local army pay records and accounts were flown back to Britain. Finally, just one Pay Corps detachment remained. In their keeping was something more precious than life to a Pay Corps man: the Command Treasury Chest.

On 10 February, the island of Singapore was under incessant shelling and bombing, and the very last convoy attempted to leave the harbour. The Pay Corps detachment embarked along with almost 2,000 other soldiers on the *Empire Star*. So did the Treasury Chest.

Thirteen Pay Corps volunteers stayed behind, as part of the force covering embarkation. All were taken by the Japanese; none were heard of again. Probably they died on the infamous Siam railway.

The *Empire Star* led a charmed life. On the first night at sea, the Japanese flew 131 sorties against her; the Pay Corps men fought the attackers off with small arms, and helped serve the ship's three-inch anti-aircraft guns. Later, the ship blundered into a minefield; somehow she emerged watertight.

Eventually, the *Empire Star* reached Djakarta, in what is now Indonesia. There, four members of the detachment and the Treasury Chest transferred to another ship. All reached England safely. Eight more men remained in Bandoeng. But the rest had acquired a taste for action. They determined to head for Australia, rather than hang about and risk capture.

At dead of night, and armed to the teeth, they advanced on the Djakarta waterfront. There, they found a grimy old collier, the SS *Wu Sang*. Her master wanted to take her to sea, but the crew – not unreasonably – thought they were safer where they were, and mutinied. The fighting accountants lent their powers of persuasion to the master. Exactly what they did is unclear; but by the time they had finished, the crew decided they would rather face sharks, bombs and torpedoes then further Pay Corps persuasion, and agreed to sail for Fremantle, near Perth.

It was certainly the strangest voyage in Pay Corps history, and one of the oddest troop movements carried out by the Army. The passenger manifest of the barely seaworthy *Wu Sang* ran roughly as follows:

'The passenger manifest of the . . . Wu Sang.'

Royal Army Pay Corps	:	one sub-detachment
War correspondents	:	10
Dancing girls	:	2
White Russian Countess	:	1

The biggest hazard of the voyage proved to be neither Japanese attacks nor drunken war correspondents, but the weather. *Wu Sang* hit storms in the Java Sea and the Indian Ocean. Twice she nearly foundered as the coal shifted. Odd torpedoes or bombs hardly seemed to matter.

It remains a matter of debate who was most surprised when, grimy and battered, the *Wu Sang* limped into Fremantle. The good citizens of Western Australia, suffering from invasion panic, almost opened fire; the crew had long since written off their fate to their Gods, and their bodies to the sharks; the war correspondents had given up hope of ever writing another expenses chit; and the dancing girls were resigned to ending up in the white slave traffic. Much Swan Lager got drunk in Perth that day.

Oddly, the doughty deeds of the accountants in khaki are known to few civilian members of the profession. The Pay Corps and the Chartered Institute have drifted apart, and – except in time of war, when called-up chartered accountants swell the ranks of the Corps – there is little contact between the two. Much closer links now exist between the Corps and other professional bodies, like the Institute of Cost and Management Accountants, and the Chartered Institute of Secretaries.

The rift seems to date back to a bizarre (or perhaps far-sighted – who can tell?) experiment in 1919. In that year, the government – worried as always by the tendency of military spending to run out of control – ordered the formation of a new Corps of Military Accountants. All its officers were to be professionally qualified chartered accountants. The idea was to impose a new system of objective accounting on the armed forces.

Alas, a compromise early on led to the new system (and the Military Accountants) operating in parallel with earlier systems (and the Pay Corps). In those Darwinian times, the fittest was supposed to survive, while the other one just withered away.

As anyone might have guessed, it didn't work out that way at all. Peppery old colonels fresh from the Great War lost no time making the new Unit Accountants' lives a misery, both in and out of the officers' mess. They resented being spied upon (as they saw it) and

'. . . a new Corps of Military Accountants.'

feared that their military skills might be judged by their financial efficiency.

In public, the Pay Corps adopted a stance of co-operative neutrality. But you can bet that in private, they provided the old soldiers with much ammunition. Moreover, the Pay Corps held a strongly persuasive lever: it handled officers' accounts. So few poorly paid junior officers wanted to upset them.

After only two years, it became clear that the experiment was failing. So the government did what it always does: it formed a committee – or, rather, a series of committees. Most splendidly – for students of Sir Humphrey and his methods – one committee delivered only one recommendation. After taking much evidence, and spending many hours deliberating, it concluded, firmly and resoundingly, that the Army Council should set up another committee.

Most of the committees included civilian accountants as members. Perfectly properly, they fought to tighten up the loose structure of Army accounting, putting it even more definitively in the hands of the Military Accountants.

That, of course, had exactly the opposite effect to what they intended. Attitudes hardened, and the Military Accountants found that their job changed from difficult to totally impossible. In 1925, the Corps of Military Accountants (then numbering 99 officers and 666 men) gave up and disbanded. About half the officers and a quarter of the men were absorbed into the Pay Corps; the rest returned to civilian life, where they said scurrilous things about soldiers.

The Corps of Military Accountants must rank among the shortest-lived regiments in the British Army. Yet the breach it caused echoes down the decades. To this day, the otherwise admirable library of the Institute of Chartered Accountants includes no copy of the Pay Corps regimental history, nor of its regular Journal.

This is a pity. For even articled clerks must sometimes wonder whether a life of grey-suited, sober-minded anonymity is going to satisfy their adventurous instincts. Closer links with their military colleagues and their glorious past (not to mention their technically adventurous present) might help them adjust to their lot, and perhaps even prevent them throwing bottles at Twickenham or Lord's.

Their fantasies, for instance, might take them with the Pay Corps to the evacuation of France in 1940. Then, in the true spirit of accountancy, men of the Corps risked their lives to protect the money.

During the 'phoney war', the Command Pay Office had finally settled in Rouen, after a spell in the casino at Pornichet. Luckily, the roulette wheels were already in store – otherwise the troops might have gone short of money.

At first, all the usual things went wrong. Accounts records for officers posted to France went to the Middle East, and vice versa; simple items of stationery (like pens) had to be 'acquired' – the Corps showed great initiative, says the official historian. Some of the emergency stores included items dating from the Boer War, including huge brass-bound ledgers and cash books. One packing case contained nothing but eyeshields; another was full of butchers' equipment.

Finally, it all settled down, and a proper Command Pay Office began making paperwork in Rouen. Hearing this, Hitler decided to over-run the low countries and northern France, and sent the Pay Corps soldiers scurrying for their port of evacuation, St Nazaire. There, they had the bad luck to be taken off by the SS Lancastria; with 5,000 soldiers aboard, she was grossly overcrowded. At 3pm on 19 June, German bombers attacked her. She sank soon afterwards; only 1,000 survived. But among them were Pay Corps men still clinging to cash boxes and moneybelts. One, a Paymaster, was rescued after many hours in the sea. He was carrying 90,000 francs; he wasn't going to let them go after marching with them all the way from Le Mans (where they had been earmarked for paying civilian labour).

If our dreaming articled clerk prefers the romance of distant lands, he can travel in his mind to Nepal. There, old Gurkha soldiers march over the mountains for many days to temporary cash offices staffed by an expeditionary force from the Pay Corps. The pensions must get through.

Or he could wish himself behind enemy lines with a special fighting detachment of the Pay Corps in what was then Palestine. Even now, their purpose remains shrouded in the fog of war. Perhaps they had secret orders to launch a devastating attack on the enemy's currency, following through with a pincer movement on bank deposits.

Fanciful? Not entirely, for one minor task of the Pay Corps in action was to provide packets of foreign currency for use on clandestine missions behind enemy lines. This is not as simple as it sounds; in the Far East, for instance, special troops carried Siamese ticals, French Indo-Chinese piastres, imperial sovereigns, and an obsolete version of Indian rupees, much valued for their high silver content. If the banknotes came clean and fresh from London stocks, the Pay Corps spent time and effort making them grubby; a new note in that part of the world would have immediately created suspicion. Whether the notes or the Pay Corps soldiers were more distressed is hard to say; khaki accountants, like their civilian brothers, are trained to respect money.

And how they respected it! Before we allow the Pay Corps to stand down, let us remember – with pride and astonishment – their part in the D-Day landings, and the fighting that followed.

The British government believed that the French commercial system would break down – or be destroyed – as battles raged across the country. So the Pay Corps set up what was, in effect, a complete mobile banking system, based on French francs.

Soon after D-Day, the first cash boxes went ashore: almost five million francs, to cover the first fortnight of operations. When the Base Cashier arrived a few weeks later, he disembarked with five and a half tons of currency, totalling 335m francs. All told, 65½ tons of currency – worth about £300m in today's money – went over the beaches or through the Mulberry Harbour. Not one franc went missing.

By September, the Corps had handled currency worth more than one billion pounds at today's values. It had been landed, transported, exchanged, paid out, collected and reconciled. Losses, say the Corps proudly, were negligible.

'. . . Khaki accountants . . .
trained to respect money.'

FOR ACCOUNTANTS' EYES ONLY

THE BOTTOM LINE

ACCOUNTS, ACCOUNTANTS AND ACCOUNTING PRINCIPLES

An understanding of accounts is what separates accountants from everybody else. Non-accountants can be divided into those to whom accounts are nothing more than a totally incomprehensible and random assortment of figures, and those who, although untrained, *think* they can understand.

Only those who have experienced the incalculable joy of having a trial balance add up first time can appreciate the full meaning of a 'balance' sheet. All those hours sweating over the £1 difference – after all, it might be two compensating errors, £1 million one way and £999,999 the other.

To the uninitiated the balancing of a trial balance first time may be broadly compared with making 7 no-trumps doubled vulnerable or alternatively making an unbeaten century – something which no matter how many times it occurs is always as good as the first time.

Knowing why your trial balance doesn't is where accountants are able to demonstrate their magical gifts with numbers. Remember all those differences which divide by 9 which indicate a transposition error, or 99 which shows that a figure on the window side in pounds has been entered on the door side in pence? Do this at the right moment (i.e. when the client is watching) and the audit will be secure for life.

'The auditors have balanced the books sir, and have gone round head office on a lap of honour.'

One famous accountancy tale concerns the senior partner, who every morning, followed the same ritual. He sat at his desk, opened a top drawer, glanced inside, closed it and began work.

When he retired, his staff rushed to see what was in the drawer. A picture of an old flame? A mantra? A rude drawing?

None of these. It was a yellowing piece of paper. On it was typed: 'Assets are on the side of the balance sheet nearest the window'.

'Old accountants never die. . . They just lose their balance.'

'Cost' is a term well known to the layman. It means everything to an accountant; that is to say it can mean everything he wants it to, depending upon the circumstances. It can mean just the cost of the materials, but there again it can include direct labour, and possibly attributable overheads; if you are really desperate it can include a proportion of head office expenses of almost any amount.

All these items form the basis of 'management accounts' which are obviously those prepared for the purposes of the management.

Unfortunately, management has a number of different purposes and the accountant (particularly if he is employed) has to satisfy them all. The figures must be capable of providing good news, bad news, or a bit of both with indications each way for those unwilling to take sides. The only problem facing the accountant is to avoid giving the impression that the management accounts can ever be reconciled to the financial accounts. The very idea is heresy; no acknowledgement of the possibility must be admitted. Management accounts must be described as 'tools of management' – not mere historic summaries. They are of course prepared in a fashion to suit the company's particular purpose, e.g. seasonally adjusted or calendarised (or hospitalised or any other long word), not the stereotype of SSAPs etc; any obvious and serious differences have to be explained by 'accounting adjustments of a technical nature'. That is not to say that the final accounts cannot themselves be subject to considerable variation.

GOODWILL

Goodwill is another concept which plays havoc with the untrained mind because non-accountants think they know what it means. Goodwill of course, as every accountant knows, means anything. It may be little more than an arithmetical difference when you have paid too much for a business. You can call the excess goodwill; the more you pay, obviously the more valuable the business was. The fact that the existence of goodwill is then immediately denied by writing it off to reserves is explained away in highly technical jargon with the blame being laid wholly at the door of statements of accounting practice.

Accountancy firms themselves are said to have goodwill. The older partners understand this as the right to the super profits. The younger partners regard it as something akin to extortion. By the time the younger partners become older partners, they are able to grasp the concept fully and cannot understand why their new younger partners object to paying for it.

'I think it's time, Miss Prideau, for our annual revaluation of goodwill.'

ETHICS

This is not a problem, specifically confined to accountants. The following story, however, gives an idea of the thorny questions involved:

> 'Dad,' said the accountant's son, 'what's ethics?'
>
> His father thought for a moment. 'It's the foundation of all business, son,' he said. 'Let me try to explain.
>
> 'Say someone came in to settle my bill for £100, and my partner James happened to be out.
>
> 'Just as the client is leaving, I find he's given me £10 too much. Now there's the ethical question: do I tell Jim or not?'

MATERIALITY

Materiality is another important concept. As an audit reaches its deadline, teams are told they need not bother with 'anything less than £10,000' today. A few days later it is 'nothing less than £100,000' and so on, depending upon the size of the client.

In the field of taxation, materiality usually has no application: if the amount is large enough to see, the tax man will be after it. However, accountants have taken considerable comfort from the celebrated tax case concerning the late Sir Charles Clore. He sought to emigrate shortly before his death in a vain attempt to save death duties. In considering the tax position in the Court of Appeal, Lord Templeman explained that if the arguments on behalf of Sir Charles were to prevail:

> No Capital Transfer Tax will become payable or at any rate the amount of the tax will be reduced to less than £4 million, a sum which appears almost trivial in the present context.

FROM LITTLE ACORNS

A true – but necessarily anonymous – story concerns the managing director of a public company and relates to a period when the company was somewhat less prosperous. In its early days, the bank and other lenders were naturally keen to see how the company was doing and when the company's accountant (unqualified of course) saw the size of the loss for one of the first years of trading, he or she decided that it would be a great deal better if a 'nought' was removed, thus reducing a (say) £50,000 loss which would have been regarded as unsupportable, to only a £5,000 loss which could be regarded as broadly acceptable. The auditors (who must also remain nameless) did not notice this irregularity until the following year, by which time the company's fortunes had improved sufficiently to allow the correction to be made without too much damage. The company continued to prosper and now reports profits in the millions. It is upon such a slender thread that commercial success can depend.

*'Good grief! This balance-sheet won't do − why damn it,
a child could understand it.'*

Some of the best stories are those which depend upon an inti-mate knowledge of the subject matter under consideration; the more obscure and refined the point, the more inner satisfaction is gained. Consider the following story from Ian Griffiths which, it must be said, could only be understood by an accountant, and only then by those who recall the different methods of treating extraordinary items and exceptional items. (For those who have forgotten, the story will probably remind you.)

The Finance Director one day discovers that one overseas division has made an uncharacteristic loss of £1 million. He goes to tell the Chairman who says 'How extraordinary. Let's hope it does not happen again'. The Finance Director leaves with a knowing look on his face. Minutes later he discovers that another overseas division has made an uncharacteristic profit of £1 million. Off he trots to tell the Chairman who retorts 'What an exceptional performance. Let's hope they keep it up'. Exit the Finance Director with another knowing look.

A story is told of one large firm of accountants whose senior partner was of a forceful and independent disposition – not always seeing eye to eye with his younger partners and never letting them have their way. He was legendary for ending his meeting by saying 'Those in favour say "Aye", those against say "Aye – resign" '!

*'I don't think Hankinson quite understands
the decision-making process yet.'*

A partner in a large firm of accountants was often called upon to give lectures but he tended to delegate the writing of the lectures to one of his junior staff. Being of a somewhat unpleasant disposition and quick to criticise if any error appeared in the text, this was not a task much sought after. One of his junior staff who had obviously been prevailed upon once too often set to work on what was to be his final lecture for his boss before he left the firm. On the first sheet he wrote the introduction, explaining that the subject was of great complexity but of such importance that a careful and lucid explanation of the difficult points was necessary.

That evening the partner concerned, having given his mouth-watering introduction to his subject, turned the page to be met with a blank sheet save for the words 'You're on your own now, old man'.

On a similar theme there was a well-known accountant who was in great demand to give lectures on his particular speciality and he spent a great deal of time travelling round the country driven by his loyal chauffeur. On the way to one engagement he mentioned to his chauffeur that he felt a little unwell and maybe he should give the evening a miss; he was reluctant to do so because he did not want to let the organisers down.

'Don't worry, Sir,' said the chauffeur, 'I always sit at the back of the hall and have heard your speech 100 times – I know it off by heart. Why don't we swap places and I will give your speech for you'.

'That will never work,' said the accountant, 'there are always the questions at the end'.

'That's no problem,' said the chauffeur, 'the questions are always the same you know and I have heard all the answers many times'.

Eventually the accountant was persuaded to change places and the chauffeur duly took the platform while his illustrious employer sat at the back of the hall in the chauffeur's uniform. The chauffeur delivered his speech impeccably and the questions went smoothly until a member of the audience asked a question which had never been asked before. Unperturbed the chauffeur rubbed his chin and said

'Well now, that is a very interesting question. But at the same time it is a very simple question. And just to prove how simple it is I am going to ask my chauffeur who is sitting at the back of the hall to answer it for me'.

THE AUDITOR

The fact that accountants in general and auditors in particular are regarded as pretty boring may have something to do with the nature of the work. The subject does not exactly get off to an impressive start when one looks at the definition – at least that provided by *Longman's Management Glossary.*

> **The process of verifying the accounting records of an organisation by a third party. An audit normally includes checking against original documents giving rise to the transactions which are recorded, verifying creditor and debtor balances by direct enquiry, verifying the existence and value of fixed assets.**

The traditional view of auditors and auditing is instilled into the young accountant at a very early stage of his training. No accountant will ever forget the immortal words of Lord Justice Lopes in the Kingston Cotton Mill case:

> **The auditor is a watchdog and not a bloodhound.**

'At least we've no fear of automation − a computer could never day-dream consistently for eight hours a day, five days a week.'

(which were famously rendered by an aspiring young accountant in his examination as 'The Auditor is a bulldog and not a bloody greyhound').

Why is it that these words conjure up the image of a lumbering plodder and not, as one might expect, the image of someone constantly vigilant and alert, ready to spring into action the moment his suspicion is roused – as every good watchdog should be; surely that's what auditing is all about! Perhaps it is something to do with his Lordship's unfortunate name. Maybe everything would have been different if somebody else had tried the case – Pennycuick, J. would seem much more appropriate. But Lord Justice Lopes did not stop there; he went on to say of the duties of auditors:

Their work is responsible and laborious and their remuneration moderate.

'Miss Tribble, get me my accountant!'

That sounds rather like a death knell to any glamorous aspirations an auditor might have.

The work of an auditor makes him the target for any number of barbed comments and unflattering stories; however, anybody whose job it is to check on the accuracy of another's work is hardly likely to be welcomed with open arms. Inevitably he will discover some accounting discrepancy, much to the displeasure of those who have the privilege of paying for his services. He may not be a bloodhound but he might well ferret out the odd malpractice – were we not all taught how to spot teeming and lading and how to view with suspicion the hardworking cashier who never goes on holiday – just in case his selfless devotion is a cover for some complex false accounting. Such an uncharitable approach is hardly likely to win friends and influence people – and auditors need all the friends they can get.

'Good grief! You're both alarmingly young for auditors. I trust you're acquainted with accepted corporate accounting principles.'

However, it does seem a little harsh for the auditor to be described so often in the following glowing terms:

A man who goes in after the battle is over to count the dead and bayonet the wounded.

The selection of an auditor is obviously a matter of great skill and it is something worthy of consideration at the highest level:

The directors of a major company had decided to appoint a new firm of auditors and the choice had narrowed to three firms. The Chairman called the senior partner of each firm to his office and explained that each would be asked a single question. It would be the same question and they would be allowed only one answer; on the basis of the answers he received he would make his decision. All three partners agreed that this was fair and they left the room to await the call.

The first auditor was called in and sat facing the entire board. They scrutinized him and finally the Chairman asked 'What is two and two?'

The auditor was a little surprised at such an elementary question but clients are not known for their numeracy so he replied 'four'. He was shown out and the next candidate was shown in.

The same procedure took place and having given the question some thought the second candidate said:

'The obvious answer is four but no doubt you want somebody who can think a little beyond the obvious; I think the answer is 22'.

He was shown out and the third auditor shown in. Again the same question was asked. 'What is two and two?' The auditor thought for a moment, looked at the Chairman and said:

'What sort of figure did you have in mind?'

He got the job.

The auditor's concentration on the historic aspects of the company's affairs can sometimes lead to accusations that he lives in an unreal world, being more concerned with the past than the future.

It has been said that a company is like a car going down a road at high speed. The managing director is doing the steering, the sales director has his foot hard on the accelerator and the finance director has his foot hard on the brake. The auditor is sitting in the back giving directions by looking at a map he has just made by looking out of the back window.

'Our auditors recommend a day of prayer!'

YOU ALWAYS REMEMBER
THE FIRST TIME

Roger Nuttall

Here's a funny thing, as Max Miller used to say. A decade ago that fine anthologist B. S. Johnson had a wonderful idea, as brilliant as it was simple. He asked celebrities to contribute tales of their first sexual encounters: happy or sad, successful or unsuccessful.

Surprisingly contributors rushed to co-operate. In his preface, Johnson says, he expected many rejections and a few successes; in fact, the famous practically fell over themselves as they clamoured to tell their tales of innocence, fear, and fumbling incompetence. It was as if they were saying: 'This is how I was; now look at me!'

What was true of sex, I thought, must also be true of money. Most of us shroud our financial lives – like our sex-lives – in shame-faced privacy. Watch the way people create a little no-go area around themselves as they cash a cheque at the bank counter. Listen to the outrage if someone dares ask a news commentator how much he earns – that same commentator who, moments before, was attacking the high pay of Members of Parliament or pop stars.

Those who have achieved the security of great riches, power or distinction (or who would like us to believe they have) must look back on their early financial gropings with the same amused tolerance as those who now see themselves as mature and sophisticated lovers. Or so I reasoned. The reality turns out to be quite different. Armed and encouraged by tales told me privately by accountants and captains of industry I asked many leaders of the profession what they remembered of their early auditing jobs, and an equal number of successful businessmen and accountants about their early confrontations with accountants.

It seemed a fertile ground to till. Thirty or forty years ago, a visiting audit was often a young articled clerk's first trip away from home – and somebody else was paying! I had heard of dreadful debauchery and the bleary-eyed consequences, of smart but shady businessmen encouraging the typing pool to divert and distract easily tempted audit clerks – even, romantically, of an illicit affair that began over the bought ledger and ended in a double dismissal, but a happy marriage.

The other side of the hill looked every bit as green. What multi-millionaire could resist the chance to look back on his early, struggling days and remember the panic that preceded his first audits? Few great businesses reach adolescence without heart-stopping moments of near-insolvency and last-minute book-fiddling – sorry, ledger adjustments. The chairman of one of our biggest companies has told me how, for three years running, he was felled by a debilitating illness in September. It was much later that he realised that the cause was not overwork, as he thought, but fear of what might turn up in the impending audit – even though, in fact, he had nothing to be afraid of.

'. . . fear of the impending audit . . .'

And, I thought, I could tie these merry tales up neatly by recalling a long-dead tradition that kept both auditors and businessmen happy. Or, at any rate, merry.

For good reasons, breweries used to end their financial year in September. Many still do. If the brewers had judged it nicely, the previous year's stock of hops and barley was exhausted, and what yuppies might now call the Burton Nouveau was about to come onto the market. It was a sensible time to rule off the books and see how they were doing.

Some time around the end of the eighteenth century, one brewer – possibly Samuel Whitbread, though there is great uncertainty – decided to celebrate the end of one brewing year and the beginning of the next by making a special strong beer: an audit ale, as it became known.*

*Some date audit ale even earlier: college breweries, they say, brewed an audit ale at the beginning of the new academic year. Whatever the truth, the effect was much the same: amnesia.

'Audit ale.'

Here, stories diverge. The brewers insist that the ale was meant to be drunk – by directors and employees – at the end of the audit, to celebrate a successful year or to drown the sorrow of an unsuccessful one.

Accountants, on the other hand, are a professionally suspicious lot. They think audit ale (which some breweries still produce) was meant to knock the accountants pie-eyed, in the hope that, thus anaesthetised, they would overlook certain errors and omissions. One way or another, however, a good time was had by all. As a ritual, this had much in common with the quarterly meetings of Adventurers held by the old Cornish tin mining companies.

Until the middle of the last century, their cost-book accounting system (like much else about Cornish mining) was unique, similar only to the books kept by ship-traders a century or two before.

In effect, each company was liquidated and re-formed every quarter (later, the accounting period was extended, sometimes to as long as a year). Every three months, those who had put up the money – the Adventurers – would journey to Cornwall to hear an account of the mine's income and expenditure, and to divide up the spoils. Before they returned, the Mine Captain – managing director, we would now call him – had to persuade them to reinvest the money he needed to finance new capital spending, and for working capital. Thus a tradition grew up of splendid, if drunken, Adventurers' dinners held at a local inn. Captains reasoned that if you poured enough good claret and port into the Adventurers, they would say yes to anything, and certainly fail to notice the more questionable items in the quarter's accounts.

To this day, many Cornish inns preserve the elaborate dinner services made for Adventurers' dinners. Usually, the name of the mine and an improving motto is engraved on the two biggest pieces: the wine jug – and the chamber pot.

'The wine jug – and the chamber pot.'

Alas, audits are no longer such fun for either side. Even so, I looked forward to hearing and passing on the ribald and rumbustious memories of senior accountants and famed financiers.

I have to report that I can do no such thing. I asked some thirty-five people to contribute. Far from falling over themselves in the rush, only one agreed to be quoted. It would be unfair to let his (embarrassing) story stand in isolation. Another half-dozen offered stories, but only on the condition that they were to be used anonymously, if at all.

One – from the tax partner of one of our greatest firms – bears repeating, even on those conditions. As an articled clerk of only a few months' standing, he was sent North on a big audit. 'I had hardly any idea of what was expected of me,' he told me. 'I think I was meant to be a gofer for the team of four who did the audit.'

We were meant to be taken from our cheapish hotel to the company headquarters in a hired car. On the first morning (having arrived late the previous evening) I went into the lobby at 8.30, as instructed. A little later, some older chaps came down. 'Ah,' they said, 'you must be the new lad'. Indeed I was, so I latched on to them gratefully and went with them to work.

It was four days before I found that (1) I was helping audit the wrong company; (2) I was working for the firm we regarded as our biggest rivals; and (3) one of the other firm's articled clerks had been doing my job.

In retrospect, I can see all kinds of ways in which I might have turned the situation to advantage. In effect, I had swapped identities with another young chap of much the same age and background.

Unfortunately, at the time, I was in far too great a panic. I arranged to meet my opposite number, who was all for coming clean at once. I thought it was best to keep up the pretence for the rest of the audit and hope for the best. We tossed for it. I won. How he got on, I don't know. I didn't bump into anyone connected with that audit until several weeks later — not knowingly, at any rate. Then a complete stranger in the lift said: 'Haven't seen you since Manchester. Lost some weight since then, I see. Bet you won't forget that night in the Rialto in a hurry!'

What had been done that night in the Rialto in my name, I never found out. And to this day, I have never told the story to anyone else.

And just one — equally and sadly anonymous — story from the other side of the fence. The man concerned is now a distinguished retailer.

I was in my second job. I had just been promoted — to a very junior managership indeed — and was feeling very pleased with myself.

One day I was sitting at my desk contemplating a golden future when the phone rang. It was a chap from another branch. 'They're on their way,' he said, in conspiratorial tones. I had no idea what he was talking about, and told him so. 'The auditors,' he said, impatiently. 'We always give you a bell when they're on the way, so you can do the necessary.'

This still didn't mean much to me. But I thought I had better go to the entrance hall to see these auditors in, whoever they might be.

'. . . their faces fell and they pushed past me angrily.'

As I got down, two men — clearly accountants, from their sober clothes and briefcases — were about to enter.

Being a polite sort of chap, I opened the glass door for them, saying something like: 'Good morning, gentlemen, we were expecting you'.

To my surprise, their faces fell and they pushed past me angrily.

It was only later that I discovered I had wrecked a system that had worked admirably for years. We

had a fairly primitive book-keeping system, and many original records were kept at local offices.

By agreement with head office, teams from the auditors were supposed to drop in on these offices unannounced. It was meant to keep us on our toes.

But accountants are creatures of routine and habit, and their route from branch to branch was well-established. So an early warning system had grown up. As soon as the accountants left one branch, a junior manager would telephone the next to say they were coming.

When they arrived, you were supposed to act surprised. Meanwhile, of course, you had valuable time to get things ship-shape and up to date.

It was an excellent system, and my colleagues never forgave me for letting the cat out of the bag.

Two tales, when I had hoped for thirty-five. What should we make of this?

I conclude that we are happy to admit past sexual incompetence, because we believe (rightly or wrongly) that we learn from experience. We don't admit past financial incompetence, because we fear we do not!

ACCOUNTANTS AND THE ARTS

KEVIN
WOODCOCK

Creative artists and money don't mix. Sometimes they just can't be
bothered with it, sometimes it baffles them – and, too frequently,
they hand it to someone else to manage who proves fraudulent.

On the whole, artists are surprisingly sympathetic to accountants.
Artists and writers see accountants as the shield that stands between
them and the forked spear of the taxman.

Hilaire Belloc's experience was (we must hope) typical. Clearly he
received much good advice from his own accountant. For, when Ethel
Smythe was about to turn professional, he wrote to her:

> I will tell you with rapidity and lucidity what to do
> in the matter of income tax when you are a profes-
> sional. Be at the pains of putting down every single
> item of expenditure whatsoever every day which
> could possibly be twisted into a professional ex-
> pense: and remember to lump in all the doubtfulls.

On the following pages, you can read what other artists and writers
have to say about the profession.

BARRY FANTONI

Because I work from home most of the time, my accountant, Mr Allen (I have changed his name because this story might not do him a lot of good) comes to see me when it is time to 'go over the books'. He is, by the way, also my wife's accountant.

The last time he came, his visit coincided with the arrival of another cocker spaniel to our already crowded home. The appointment was for 4pm. He was on time but I had been unexpectedly called out and had got stuck in traffic.

I am told that when Mr Allen arrived, the new dog took an immediate fancy to his trouser leg. In fact, Archie, our new cocker, would not let go of dear Mr Allen. My wife offered tea and Mr Allen politely said that he would love a cup. Archie was delighted. As soon as Mr Allen sat down Archie was on him

K. Lamb

in a flash. The tea went everywhere, but mainly over Mr Allen's trousers.

Shock. Horror. My wife at once insisted she took his wet trousers to dry off upstairs. Very reluctantly, Mr Allen agreed. He was given a dressing gown and to avoid any further risk with Archie, took refuge on the landing outside our bedroom.

What with the trousers and Archie and the spilled tea, they had forgotten about my impending arrival.

Poor Mr Allen, a dry, well-mannered man; a friend of the family — found lurking, when I opened the front door, on the landing outside our bedroom dressed in my dressing gown and no trousers. These were of course in my wife's hands.

If my bank statement showed that I was in the red, it was nothing compared to the colour of dear Mr Allen's face.

ROBERT MORLEY *(Responsible Gentlemen)*

> Like most actors I have been in continuous dispute, if that is the phrase, with Her Majesty's Commissioners of Inland Revenue ever since she came to the throne. Before that I had the same trouble with her father's and with his father's, come to that. But I don't wish to dwell on the subject.

JOHN MORTIMER *(Two starts for comfort)*

> And what have I achieved? Three women in my life and one of *them* turned out to be a Chartered Accountant.

When Noël Coward was asked whether it was the £1,000 per week which had lured him to appear in Cabaret at the Café de Paris, the master had the complete response:

> When the Gentlemen of the Treasury have had their cut, not forgetting the extra 4d on National Insurance, my accountant has assured me that I can count on not less than 30 shillings for the four weeks.

(The Wit of Noël Coward)

GLENDA JACKSON *(Tolley's Practical Tax)*

> My money goes to my agent, then to my accountant and from him to the tax man.

CHRISTOPHER WARD *(How to Complain)*

> Would you engage in conversation in Swahili with a nuclear physicist on the subject of thermodynamics? If not, what makes you feel you are

qualified to discuss your financial affairs with one of Her Majesty's Inspectors of Taxes?

Disputes between ordinary mortals and those civil servants employed to fill the nation's purses are best left to those who speak the language and understand the game: accountants.

'I always had the feeling you'd excel at figures.'

CHARLES DICKENS

Mr Micawber in *David Copperfield* had a very astute financial brain but he was obviously no accountant. It may be recalled that he said

> Annual income 20s — Annual expenditure 19s 6d — result: happiness
>
> Annual income 20s — Annual expenditure 20s 6d — result: unhappiness

The accountant knows better than this. He knows that if you have an annual income of 20s and your annual expenditure is 19s 6d the result is 6d: happiness has nothing to do with it.

Gilbert and Sullivan may have left auditors off the Lord High Executioner's list but in connection with Koko's marriage immediately afterwards Poohbah talks about how he will advise him in his many 'Lord High' capacities:

> Of course, as First Lord of the Treasury, I would propose a special vote that would cover all expenses if it were not that, as Leader of the Opposition, it would be my duty to resist it, tooth and nail. Or, as Paymaster-General, I could so cook

the accounts that as Lord High Auditor I should never discover the fraud. But then as Archbishop of Titipu it would be my duty to denounce my dishonesty and give myself into my own custody as First Commissioner of Police.

THREE LITTLE ACCOUNTANTS FROM SCHOOL ARE WE...

K.Lamb

THE OLD ENEMIES

THE BOTTOM LINE

Accountants owe a great deal to William Pitt. When on 3 December 1798 he rose to deliver his Budget speech (he was at the time combining the offices of Prime Minister and Chancellor of the Exchequer) and imposed Income Tax for the first time – at least in its present form – he could not have foreseen the consequences: the development of the accountancy profession into the field of taxation and the skills which are now so expensively sought.

These days accountants and taxation tend to be thought of in the same breath (much to the chagrin of the legal profession, it seems) and inevitably there are a growing number of accountants who think about little else. Given the incredibly arcane nature of the subject which by right should be regarded as infinitely more boring than auditing, it is quite extraordinary that tax advisors have a more glamorous image. Possibly it is because paying tax is the bane of almost everybody's life and if the accountant does his stuff the result is a saving in real money – you don't get the same direct correlation of cost and benefit with auditing. Another reason may be that tax has been an emotive subject for centuries (remember John Hampden and Ship Money, not to mention the Boston Tea Party) and anybody who helps, or even tries to help, John Citizen to beat the bureaucratic steamroller must be on to a good thing. Someone famous might well have said that it is a truth universally acknowledged that a single man in possession of a good fortune must be in want of a good tax advisor.

It is in the field of tax that the accountant breaks free of his traditional image and becomes thought of as some kind of guru, constantly outwitting the Inland Revenue in the annual ritual which surrounds the assessment and collection of tax. How this has occurred is nothing short of remarkable particularly because the truth is often otherwise. The reason must be that to the client, tax is even more of a mystery than accounting (at least accounts have some underlying logic) and even if the Inland Revenue have trampled all over the accountant the client would probably never know – or even understand.

This mysterious quality perhaps derives from the fact that accountants have to grapple with the strangest and most contorted forms of words which can be imagined – and worse. Pity the poor accountant whose client is concerned with ground nuts, for if he is to advise on the VAT position he will have to try to make sense of the following:

In the Nuts (unground) (other than ground nuts) Order, the expression nuts shall have reference to such nuts other than ground nuts as would but for this amending order not qualify as nuts (unground)

(other than ground nuts) by reason of their being nuts (unground).

Anybody who can get to grips with that must be nuts.

Various efforts have been made over the years to simplify the drafting of tax legislation but there would still seem to be room for improvement if the following is anything to go by:

Take notice that by virtue of Regulation 27A of the Income Tax (Employments) Regulations 1973 as inserted by Regulation 5 of the Income Tax (Employments) (No. 15) Regulations 1985, Regulation 8A of the Income Tax (Sub-Contractors in the Construction Industry) Regulations 1975 as inserted by Regulation 4 of the Income Tax (Sub-Contractors in the Construction Industry) Regulations 1985 and Regulation 27A inserted in Schedule 1 to the Social Security (Contributions) Regulations 1979 by Regulation 3 of the Social Security (Contributions) Amendment Regulations 1985 . . .

and so it goes on.

The tax collector started as he meant to go on. John Horne Tooke received the 17th-century equivalent of an estimated assessment: He made the following reply:

I have much more reason than the Commissioners can have to be dissatisfied with the smallness of my income. I have never yet in my life deserved or had occasion to reconsider any declaration which I have signed with my name. But the Act of Parliament has removed all the decencies which used to prevail among gentlemen and has given the Commissioners (shrouded under the signature of their clerk) a right by law to tell me that they have reason to believe that I am a liar. They also have right to demand from me, upon oath, the particular circumstance of my private situation. In obedience to the law, I am ready to attend upon this degrading occasion so novel to an Englishman and give them every explanation they may be pleased to require.

'Really, both your lads are at Eton, are they?'

A question often on the lips of those concerned with taxation, is the difference between 'tax avoidance' and 'tax evasion'. It is as well to remember which is which (for those who have forgotten, 'avoidance' is considered O.K.), having regard to the following explanation of the distinction, said to have been uttered by Denis Healey:

> The difference between tax avoidance and tax evasion is the thickness of a prison wall.

Whenever the tax man gets into difficulty in charging a tax he can always resort to the age-old device of a 'deeming'. Where else but in taxation could you expect to find the following:

> In this paragraph 'year' means the period beginning with 27th March 1974 and ending with 5th April 1974.

Schedule 6(2)(3) Finance Act 1975.

*'It was a nightmare come true –
my accountant was a VAT double agent.'*

These sentiments have also been judicially expressed by no less a person than Lord Justice Singleton (*Briggenshaw v Crabb, 30 TC 331*):

Your appeal must be dismissed. I will pass you back your documents. If I might add a word to you, it is that I hope you will not trouble your head further with tax matters, because you seem to have spent a lot of time in going through these various Acts, and if you go on spending your time on Finance Acts and the like, it will drive you silly.

The relationship between accountants and Inspectors of Taxes is always odd. Both try to ensure that tax is not paid unless it is properly due, but rarely agree on what is properly due.

'It's a company car.'

Correspondence with the Inland Revenue sometimes has the mark of the fanciful about it. But the following letter from an accountant to the Inland Revenue on behalf of his client seems to contain the flavour of authenticity:

In reply to your letter of 12th instant, there is no documentary evidence of partnership, but when I called at my client's premises to complete the Tax Return his wife was present, and when I asked if the business belonged to him, his wife immediately answered in the most forthright terms that it was their joint property, and I personally was sufficiently convinced not to pursue the matter further. I take some pride in my physical condition, but I know my limitations, and if you are still not convinced I will take you along in my car to see Mrs X with pleasure, but I will wait outside for you.

'Dammit Sam! I expect my accountant to contribute a bit more than "it's a fair cop".'

The following delightful letter was received by the Inland Revenue from an accountant acting for one of his impoverished but aristocratic clients:

We know very well that our client lives in a frugal manor.

'For a start I suggest you cut down on your life-style.'

One well-known aristocrat, told by his accountant to economise by using buses instead of taxis, telephoned the latter to say 'I took your advice and got on a bus after leaving your office – told it to go to Carlton Terrace and it went nowhere near the place!'

The tax return will be undergoing a profound change next year as the Government continue their plans for simplification of the tax system. Instead of the long and incomprehensible form, a shorter form will be issued with the following message:

1. How much money did you make last year?
2. How much have you got left?
3. Send it.

'Let's put it this way. . . how much have you got?'

I cannot say whether Baroness Phillips lives frugally or otherwise. But she has had her share of embarrassment. She recalls:

> I was travelling with an old friend, a college principal, to an educational conference at which we were both speakers. In conversation I mentioned that my accountant had just frightened me to death by telling me I will be brought before the Commissioners if I do not complete my tax returns and I can just imagine them – a group of hardfaced old inquisitors. My companion smiled:
>
> 'Actually,' she said, 'I am a Tax Commissioner'.

Mortimer Caplan too has no doubts on the subject:

> There is one difference between a tax collector and a taxidermist — the taxidermist leaves the hide.

In literature and elsewhere there is much to support the words of Edmund Burke in 1774 when he said:

> To tax and to please, no more than to love and to be wise, is not given to man.

and again in 1780:

> Taxing is an easy business. Any projector can contrive new compositions, any bungler can add to the old.

Winston Churchill remarked in 1937:

> There is no such thing as a good tax.

Ernest Hemingway on receiving a $100,000 tax demand in 1941:

> If anyone asks the children what their father did in the war they can say he paid for it.

The Duke of Edinburgh's view is certainly worth considering:

All money nowadays seems to be produced with a natural homing instinct for the Treasury.

Will Rogers' views on tax are certainly pertinent:

It has made more liars out of American people than golf.

Perhaps we should leave the last words on tax to Benjamin Franklin:

There are two certain things in this world — death and taxes.

('and death, thank God, doesn't get any worse'. Anon)

EXTRAORDINARY ITEMS

This chapter is entitled Extraordinary Items because it contains everything which could not conveniently be grouped under any other heading. This is not a new experience; I remember as an articled clerk analysing endless cash books where most of the expenditure seemed to end up in miscellaneous expenses – at least until I learned where they ought to go. Others used to put such items into a suspense account but that seemed to achieve very little – after all, everybody knows that items in a suspense account have to be re-analysed somewhere else, whereas you could lose a lot in miscellaneous. My more sophisticated colleagues used to divide up such items into 'sundry expenses', general expenses' and 'miscellaneous expenses' – between these three items you could put almost everything. However, the clients never seemed to be particularly happy to find practically the whole of their annual expenditure described in such vague terms – although it must have been a great comfort to those clients who only seemed to be interested in discussing the miscellaneous expenses, ignoring such things as a catastrophic fall in the gross profit percentage.

This may be the reason why accountants have their own version of Parkinson's Law which is known as the Law of Triviality:

The time spent in discussing any item in the accounts will be in inverse proportion to its size.

Reginald Taylor FCA provides some interesting correspondence:

In October 1986 I received a letter from a firm of solicitors in Hertfordshire. I had written to them for details of our client's acquisition of a property and their explanation left me no doubt about the position. It contained the following passage.

By a conveyance dated 29th May 1933 the house conveyed to Mr John Smith and his brother Mr James Smith the consideration being £1500. The parties were joint tenants and the property vested in Mr John Smith by survivorship on 9th March 1934 on which date Mr James Smith was eaten by a tiger.

And they say accountants have no sense of humour.

BEWARE OF THE CAT

'Another happy failure.'

It was the height of the secondary banking crisis of the early seventies. The Bank of England was conducting urgent talks to set up the 'lifeboat' system, designed to prevent a collapse of secondary banking pulling down some of the major circulating banks as well. Present at these discussions was Sir Kenneth Cork, senior partner of Cork, Gully & Co.

It was two o'clock in the morning and the great iron doors clanged to one after another. As Sir Kenneth was shown out by the Wicket Gate, 'for heaven's sake', said the senior official, 'pull down your hat and put up your collar! If you're seen leaving here at this time of night the pound won't stand much chance tomorrow'.

'Baroyds' bank? . . . Snooks Engineering Limited here . . . help!'

Mr Michael Checkland FCA, Director-General of the BBC, tells of the parent company which insisted that one of its less successful subsidiaries reduce its losses in the next financial year from £200,000 to £100,000. At the halfway stage the Financial Controller was surprised to receive a call from the subsidiary 'have already achieved this year's target loss of £100,000: await your further instructions'.

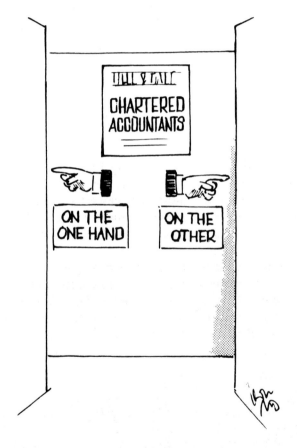

The most corny accountancy story concerns the businessman who placed an advertisement in a newspaper for a one-armed accountant. When his friend enquired why he particularly wanted an accountant with only one arm he replied:

' I am absolutely fed up with my present accountant. All he ever says is "On the one hand you can do this and on the other . . ." '

The accountant's unfortunate reputation is perhaps based on this kind of story:

A tramp was selling matchboxes outside Westminster Underground Station but trade was very slack. As a politician approached, the man called out:

'Please buy a box of matches guv'nor,' he said. 'I haven't eaten for three days'.

The politician explained to him the difficulties surrounding the economic situation but said that it would pick up shortly and next week his situation would be improved.

An accountant approached and again the tramp called out:

'Please buy a box, only 10p – I haven't sold any for a whole week'.

The accountant stopped and enquired of the man:

'And how does that compare with the same period last year?'

Nevertheless accountancy can offer some speedy and advantageous career moves. Consider a firm's promotion prospects in the light of the potentially precarious position of its Financial Director.

a) If the Financial Director is really good he will be headhunted – leaving a vacancy.

b) If he is really bad he will be fired – leaving a vacancy.

c) If the company prospers the Financial Director may well land the top job – leaving a vacancy.

d) If the company is doing badly, the Financial Director will know first and will leave before anybody else finds out – leaving a vacancy.

e) If the Managing Director dies or is assassinated, only the Financial Director has a sufficient familiarity with all aspects of the business to take over – leaving a vacancy.

'I went on an ego trip once and nobody noticed.'

Perhaps the most famous accountancy story is that concerning the hot air balloon:

Two men are in a hot air balloon and are progressing nicely when they inadvertently enter a cloud. When they emerge they can find no correlation at all between their map and the terrain below. However, seeing a man walking his dog a long way below, they swoop down towards him in the hope of obtaining some assistance. As they near the ground one of the balloonists shouts out:

'Excuse me, can you tell us where we are please?'

The man looks up and shouts 'You're in a balloon'.

At that moment a gust of wind sweeps them away, rendering any continuing conversation impossible.

The other balloonist turns to his companion and says:

'Of all the people we had to find, it had to be a chartered accountant'.

'How on earth do you know that?' said the other.

'Well, the information he gave us was absolutely accurate but it was totally useless.'

The prize for the most unfortunate name must go to the Government. They decided some years ago to establish a Government accountancy service so that the Government could be supplied with all the necessary accountancy expertise. All Government departments get reduced to acronyms and they should have been able to foresee that the head of the Government accountancy service would inevitably end up as 'Hotgas'.

One person who seemed to fare quite well in his battles with the Inland Revenue without the need of an accountant was Mr Albert Haddock, the litigious creation of A.P. Herbert.

In the celebrated case of *Haddock v Board of Inland Revenue* he successfully claimed a deduction for sunlight treatment, foreign foods and wine and attendance at Monte Carlo and Cowes for the purpose of nourishing his brain, which he regarded as an author's plant and machinery.

Perhaps Mr Haddock's most famous case was *Rex v Haddock* in which he sought to pay his tax bill by tendering a cheque written on a cow. The cheque was rejected by the Collector of Taxes on the grounds that it could not be paid into the bank but this argument was rejected because he could have endorsed it on the back (or in this case on the underneath). The cow was not 'crossed' but was an open cow and the only reason why it was not endorsed was because it had taken up a menacing posture, obviously resenting the idea of endorsement. This represented insufficient grounds for rejecting the payment and (naturally) Mr Haddock won his case.

'The one in the grey suit is the author. The others are accountants.'

It seems unlikely that accountants will ever become glamorous heroes to compare with the Lone Ranger, Rumpole or even Robin Hood – although come to think of it even he could be regarded as an embryonic tax planner, what we professionals call an income alienation specialist. The best we seemed to manage was a young lady called Heather who made a brief appearance in 'Brookside' (whatever that is) but then sank without trace. However, it seems unlikely that the need for the services of unglamorous accountants will subside, at least not until some born-again Pacioli comes up with a new system. This prospect may not enable us to get much of a laugh out of life, but at least it looks as though we will probably always have a job.